FROM BEAN TO BEAN PLANT

Anita Ganeri

Heinemann Library
Chicago, Illinois

Customer Service 888-454-2279
Visit our website at www.heinemannraintree.com

Designed by Ron Kamen and edesign
Printed in China

15 14 13 12
10 9 8 7

Library of Congress Cataloging-in-Publication Data
Ganeri, Anita, 1961-
   From bean to bean plant / Anita Ganeri, author.
      p. cm. -- (How living things grow)
   Includes bibliographical references.
   ISBN 1-4034-7861-9 (library binding - hardcover) -- ISBN 1-4034-7870-8 (pbk.)
   ISBN 978-1-4034-7861-0 (library binding - hardcover) -- ISBN 978-1-4034-7870-2 (pbk.)
  1. Fava bean--Juvenile literature. 2. Fava bean--Development--Juvenile literature. 3. Beans--Juvenile literature. 4. Beans--Development--Juvenile literature. I. Title. II. Series.
   QK495.L52.G33 2006
   583'.74--dc22
                                    2005026925

Acknowledgments
The author and publishers are grateful to the following for permission to reproduce copyright material: Ardea pp. **4**, **11**, **12**, **17**, **29**; Corbis p. **7** (Patrick Johns); FLPA pp. **5**, **10**, **25**; GPL pp. **6** (John Swithinbank), **26** (Michael Howes); Harcourt Education pp. **18** (Trevor Clifford), **21** (Chris Honeywell), **22** (Chris Honeywell); Holt Studios pp. **8**, **9**, **14**, **15**, **23**, **24**, **27**, **29**; naturepl.com pp. **20**; Photolibrary.com p. **13**; Science Photo Library p. **16** (Moira C. Smith).

Cover photograph of a bean pod reproduced with permission of Alamy Images/Carole Hallett.

Illustrations by Martin Sanders.

Some words are shown in bold, **like this**. You can find out what they mean by looking in the glossary.

Contents

Have You Ever Eaten Beans?

A bean is a type of **seed**. It grows inside a case called a **pod.** The bean grows into a new bean plant. There are many kinds of beans.

These are some of the kinds of beans we cook and eat.

You are going to learn about fava beans. You will learn how a bean seed grows into a bean plant, makes new seeds, and dies. This is the bean's life cycle.

These beans are fava beans.

Bean Seeds

Bean **seeds** grow in the ground. Some beans fall out of **pods** from old bean plants. They stay in the ground over the winter. These seeds start to grow when the weather gets warmer.

Each seed can grow into a bean plant.

Farmers plant bean seeds in rows.

Farmers collect some bean seeds.
They plant the seeds in their fields in
the spring. They water the beans
to make them grow.

Sprouting Seeds

The bean **seeds** start to grow in the spring. Parts that will grow into a new plant are in the bean.

The bean is a store of food for the new plant.

*Rain makes the
growing start.*

The way the seeds start to grow is called **germination**. The seeds need sunlight and water to make them grow.

9

Roots and Shoots

First, the **seed**'s hard case breaks open. Then, a tiny **root** grows out of the seed. The root grows down into the soil.

The root helps to fix the plant in the soil.

The shoot is bent at first. Then, it straightens out.

The next part of the plant to grow is a tiny **shoot**. It grows up through the soil into the light. It has tiny **leaf buds** at the end.

11

Growing Bigger

Over the next few weeks, the bean plant's **root** grows longer. It grows deep down into the soil. Lots of little roots grow out from the main root.

*The roots soak up water and **nutrients** from the soil.*

The **shoot** also grows straighter and taller. It is now called a **stem**. The leaves at the end of the stem start to open.

The stem takes water and food around the plant. It also holds the plant up to the light.

What do the leaves do?

13

Green Leaves

The bean plant's leaves open out and turn dark green. Like all living things, plants need food to live and grow. The leaves make this food.

The bean plants are growing well.

This picture shows how a plant makes its own food. The way a plant makes its food is called **photosynthesis**.

*The leaves take in gas (**carbon dioxide**) from the air.*

The gas and water are turned into food in the leaves.

*The roots suck up water and **nutrients** from the soil.*

The leaves take in sunlight.

15

Bean Flowers

The bean **seed** has been growing for about six to eight weeks. Flowers are starting to grow. The flowers grow from small bumps on the **stem**. These bumps are called **flower buds**.

The flower buds start to grow in the summer.

The flower buds grow all the way up the stem. They grow at the bottom of the leaves. The flowers have white petals with dark marks.

The flowers grow in big groups.

Insect Visitors

Bees and other insects visit the bean flowers. You can see them buzzing around the bean plants.

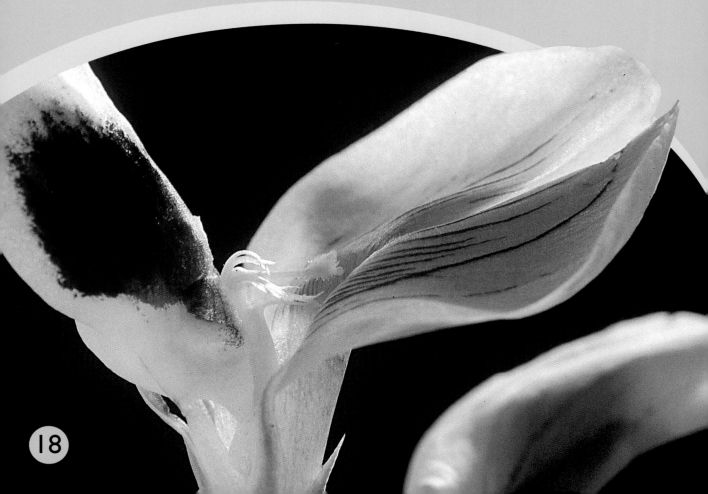

The bee has to crawl inside the flower to drink nectar.

The insects come to drink a sweet juice made by the flowers. The juice is called **nectar**. It is like an **energy** drink for insects!

19

Picking up Pollen

The flowers also make a yellow dust called **pollen**. Some of the pollen sticks to the bee as it drinks **nectar**.

This bee is covered in pollen.

Then, the bee flies to another flower to drink more nectar. There is still pollen on the insect. The pollen rubs off onto the new flower.

Bees can visit a lot of flowers in one day.

New Bean Seeds

The **pollen** from the insect joins with parts of the new flower. This is called **pollination**.

Lots of new bean seeds start to grow inside the flowers.

The new bean **seeds** are growing, so the flower's job is done. The flower's petals droop and fall off. The flower dies.

Farmers know that when the flowers die, beans are on the way.

What is a bean **pod?** 23

Bean Pods

The bean **seeds** grow in tough, thick cases. These cases are called **pods**. The pods keep the beans safe as they grow bigger.

At first, the inside of a bean pod is soft and furry. The bean seed is small and pale.

Each bean seed is joined to the inside of the pod by a short **stalk**. The stalk brings food and water from the bean plant to the bean seed.

As the bean seeds grow bigger, the pods grow longer and thicker.

Splitting Pods

In the summer, people pick some of the bean **pods**. They take the juicy bean **seeds** out of the pods. Then, they cook the beans. The beans are tasty to eat.

People keep some of the beans to plant next spring.

In the fall, the pods left on the bean plant start to turn black. Then, the plant dies. Some of the pods split open, and the beans fall to the ground.

The bean seeds will stay in the ground during the winter. They will start to grow the next spring. Then, the bean's life cycle begins again.

Life Cycle of a Fava Bean

10 Seeds fall to the ground.

1 Fava bean **seed** in the soil

2 Seed starts to grow in the spring

9 Bean plant dies in the fall

3 First **root** and **shoot** grow

8 People pick beans to eat. They keep some beans to plant.

4 **Stem** grows taller and first leaves grow

7 New seeds grow in **pods**

6 Insects **pollinate** flowers

5 Flowers open in the summer

28

Fava Bean Plant Map

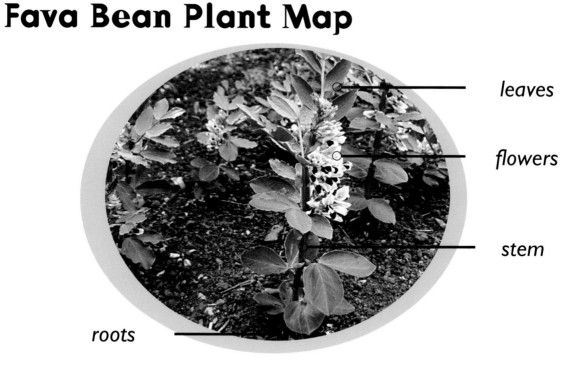

leaves

flowers

stem

roots

Fava Bean Pod Map

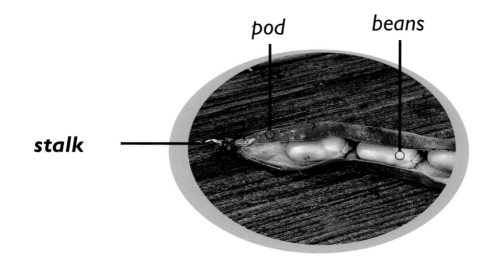

pod

beans

stalk

Glossary

carbon dioxide gas in the air

flower buds start of flowers

energy strength needed to do activities

germination how a seed starts to grow into a plant

leaf buds start of leaves

nectar sweet juice made in a flower

nutrients food living things need to grow

photosynthesis way a plant makes its own food from sunlight, gas, and water

pod case that beans grow in

pollen yellow dust made in a flower

pollinate take pollen from one flower to another

pollination how pollen joins with parts of a flower to make new seeds

root part of a plant that grows into the ground

seed part of a plant that grows into a new plant

shoot new plant's first stem and leaves

stalk short stem

stem plant's tall stalk

More Books to Read

Ganeri, Anita. *Nature's Patterns: Plant Life Cycles.* Chicago: Heinemann Library, 2005.

Royston, Angela. *Life Cycle of a Bean.* Chicago: Heinemann Library, 1998.

Saunders-Smith, Gail. *Beans.* Mankato, Minn.: Pebble, 1997.

Schwartz, David M. *Life Cycles: Bean.* Milwaukee: Gareth Stevens, 2001.

Spilsbury, Louise. *Life Cycles: Bean.* Chicago: Heinemann Library, 2005.

Watts, Barrie. *Watch It Grow: Bean.* Mankato, Minn.: Smart Apple Media, 2004.

Index